Blueprint for Business Success

Your Comprehensive Guide to Strategic Decision Making In Business

By

Lane J. Taylor

Disclaimer

The content in this book is intended solely for general informational purposes. While the author has diligently strive for accuracy, there is no assurance regarding the completeness, accuracy, or suitability of the information. The author and publisher are not accountable for any losses, damages, or injuries resulting from the utilization of this information. Readers are encouraged to seek advice from relevant professionals in their respective fields. Any reliance on the book's information is at your own risk. The author and publisher disclaim any liability for the information's use or misuse. References to third-party websites, products, or services are provided for convenience and do not imply endorsements. The author and publisher are not responsible for the content, privacy policies, or practices of external websites. Your understanding and consideration are appreciated.

About The Author

Meet Lane J. Taylor, a visionary entrepreneur and strategic thinker with a passion for guiding businesses to unprecedented success. Lane's expertise extends from team building strategies to innovative problem-solving methodologies, earning him acclaim as a trailblazer in the world of business excellence.

With a dynamic approach, Lane has empowered countless entrepreneurs and intrapreneurs to navigate the complexities of the business landscape. His insights, shared in "Blueprint for Business Success" reflect a profound understanding of growth, leadership, and the art of cultivating influential teams.

Lane's commitment to excellence is not just professional; it's personal. His journey, sprinkled with insights, challenges, and triumphs, is a testament to the principles he advocates. Dive into Lane's world, where strategic brilliance meets hands-on experience, and discover the keys to unlocking your business potential.

Get ready to be inspired, motivated, and guided by Lane J. Taylor's unique perspective on strategic success. The journey to excellence awaits—join Lane in navigating it with finesse.

Table of contents

Blueprint for Business success

Introduction

Welcome to *"Blueprint for Business Success."* I'm delighted to have you accompany me on this journey, where our focus extends beyond mere discussions of business – we're immersing ourselves in the core of what it truly takes to excel strategically.

Ever find yourself amidst a whirlwind of changes and intense competition? Well, you're not alone; that's the norm in today's business world. However, it's not merely about surviving; it's about thriving and crafting your unique success story. This book is dedicated to that pursuit. In this introduction, let's establish the foundation for something more profound than strategies and plans. It's about becoming the best version of yourself and elevating your business. Strategic excellence isn't a one-time event; it's an ongoing journey of growth and evolution that surpasses conventional tactics.

Amidst this ever-evolving landscape, who do you aspire to be? That's our starting point. We'll explore aligning your personal values with your business objectives because, let's acknowledge it, a business isn't solely about products and services; it's an extension of you.

As we progress, we'll dive deep into the nuances of strategic thought. We'll focus on self-examination as a crucial element, identifying whether you align more with the role of an intrapreneur or entrepreneur. Recognizing the importance of effectively addressing challenges, rather than letting them become burdens, is paramount.

This isn't just a guide; it's your roadmap. We're challenging the notion of the solitary entrepreneur and delving into the process of forming a team that amplifies your strengths. This involves fostering a culture that surpasses written rules, emphasizing a set of values that influence every decision.

Trust becomes your invaluable asset in this fast-paced world. We'll explore the formidable strength of dependability, discuss expanding your business, turning momentum into a strategic advantage, and yes, embracing chaos – surprising as it may sound, it is the breeding ground for innovation.

Consider this book your personalized game plan. We'll discuss creating systems to monitor your business, staying vigilant, and honing the skill of influence. You'll gain insights into overcoming formidable competitors and shaping the narrative of your success.

Are you ready to embrace the Knowledge Maverick mindset? It extends beyond acquiring knowledge; it involves mastering the arts of selling, negotiating, and influencing. We'll conclude with a guide on nurturing your capabilities and remaining resilient in the constantly evolving business landscape.

"Blueprint for Business Success" isn't merely a book; it's your ally on the journey toward achieving strategic business excellence. Let's delve in, absorb, adjust, and collectively reshape the meaning of success. Prepare to not only revolutionize your business but also undergo personal transformation. Let's bring it to fruition.

Chapter 1

Defining Your Identity

In the vast adventure of life, understanding both your personal and professional identity is akin to discovering your own North Star – a guiding force shaping your journey and narrative. Your personal identity is a complex amalgamation of experiences, values, and dreams that define the essence of who you are. It influences your responses to the world and encapsulates your passions. Imagine unraveling the layers of your personality, recognizing your strengths, and embracing your uniqueness – that's the core of defining your personal identity.

Beyond the skills listed on your resume, your professional identity acts as your personal brand in the workplace. It showcases how you navigate your field, the principles you uphold, and the lasting impact you aspire to create. It transcends mere job titles; it encapsulates the authentic professional you. Although personal and professional identities are often perceived as separate entities, they dance together, influencing each other in a dynamic rhythm. Your personal experiences subtly mold your professional self, and the challenges at work shape how you perceive yourself. It's a continuous exchange, contributing to your overall sense of self. Defining your identity is not a one-size-fits-all task; it's a journey of self-discovery, reflecting on who you are, and uncovering aspects of yourself you may not have noticed before. It's akin to finding the harmony between your personal and professional tunes, ensuring they resonate in sync.

Core values play a pivotal role in this dance, akin to the beats that hold everything together. When your personal and professional identities align with these core values, it's like finding your rhythm – a deep sense of authenticity and purpose emerges.

Imagine your identity as a river, not a stagnant pond. It evolves with every twist and turn, adapting to new experiences and challenges. It's about being flexible, growing with each opportunity, and reshaping your identity along the way. Your identity isn't just a guide; it's a compass when faced with decisions. Choices aligned with your identity don't just feel right; they weave a narrative of authenticity and purpose into your life.

Building connections goes beyond mere networking; authenticity is key, whether connecting personally or professionally. It's about being genuine, fostering relationships that go beyond the surface, and enriching your journey with meaningful interactions. So, the journey of defining your personal and professional identity isn't a destination – it's an ongoing expedition. It involves understanding who you are, aligning with your values, and embracing the dynamic nature of identity as you navigate life's dance.

In the pursuit of understanding ourselves both personally and professionally, a crucial element acts as a guiding star – aligning our personal values with the goals we set in our professional lives. This isn't just a fanciful concept; it's the secret sauce that not only makes our careers successful but deeply fulfilling. Personal values, the principles at the core of our being, become the foundation of our professional identity. It's not about keeping work separate from who we are; it's about ensuring that the work we do resonates with our core beliefs, providing our careers with authentic purpose. Understanding personal values requires introspection – recognizing the ideals and virtues that truly matter. These values aren't set in stone; they grow and evolve as we experience life. Take integrity, for example; it's not just a moral high ground but a compass guiding decisions and actions with a commitment to doing what's right. Integrating personal values into professional identity is not just a theory; it's a practical approach to work life. Our professional side shouldn't be a separate entity but a seamless extension of who we are. This alignment ensures that the work we take on isn't just a job; it's a reflection of our fundamental beliefs, creating authenticity and purpose in our careers. If we value innovation, for instance, it's not just about working in a particular industry – it's about seeking roles and projects that let our creative thinking shine.

The impact of aligning our values spills into decision-making. Every choice, big or small, becomes a reflection of our moral and ethical compass. Faced with a dilemma, personal values act as a guide, helping us weigh options based on principles that deeply matter. It's not about blindly following rules; it's a dynamic process where decisions align with overarching values.

Creating a workplace culture driven by values is essential for this alignment to thrive. Recognizing and embracing the personal values of everyone in the organization builds an environment where a real sense of belonging and purpose is felt. It's not just about diversity; it's about creating a workplace that values different perspectives and encourages us to bring our authentic selves to work. In such a setting, personal values don't just match strategic goals; they become integral in shaping the organizational culture.

When personal values align with broader business goals, it becomes a catalyst for personal and professional fulfillment. It's not just about achieving success in the traditional sense; it's about finding deep satisfaction in the work we do. When personal values resonate with the larger objectives of the organization, a beautiful blend occurs where work feels purposeful.

Navigating challenges in the dynamic business world is easier when personal values align with strategic goals. This alignment becomes a source of strength, guiding us through uncertain times. It's not about avoiding challenges; it's about facing them with a sense of purpose rooted in personal values.

Communication and recognition play crucial roles in nurturing this alignment. Companies that openly communicate their values and acknowledge the personal values of employees create a culture of openness and understanding. Regular discussions about shared values and recognizing those who embody these values contribute to an environment where alignment is not just encouraged; it's celebrated. Aligning personal values with strategic business goals is not merely a concept discussed in boardrooms. It's a transformative approach that goes beyond theory. When these elements are in harmony, success is not just achieved; careers find deep fulfillment. The synergy of personal values and strategic goals creates workplaces where authenticity and purpose are not just buzzwords but the essence of how we work and succeed. It's a holistic integration that takes us beyond conventional notions of success, making our journey both meaningful and purposeful..

Blueprint for Business success

Chapter 2

Explore Yourself as the Essential Product

Embarking on the transformative journey of self-development and continuous learning is akin to choosing a lifelong adventure – a dedicated commitment to nurturing your skills, expanding your knowledge, and cultivating a growth-oriented mindset. It transcends the mere act of hitting the books; it involves planting seeds of growth that eventually bloom into personal and professional excellence. This investment is not measured solely in dollars spent; rather, it reflects a profound dedication to your ongoing evolution.

Imagine continuous learning as the pulsating heartbeat of your personal growth, resonating with curiosity and exploration. It transcends the confines of classrooms, extending to workshops, mentorship, and hands-on projects that provide practical wisdom. The tools for self-development are diverse, ranging from formal education to unconventional avenues that ignite creativity and innovation.

Self-development isn't a solitary journey; it thrives through collaboration and benefits from the experiences of others. Engaging in mentorship and networking becomes a valuable investment, offering insights from those who've navigated similar paths. Learning from both the successes and failures of mentors and peers accelerates your growth, providing a roadmap for overcoming obstacles.

Adopting a growth mindset proves to be a game-changer. It goes beyond merely believing in your abilities; it involves viewing challenges as opportunities for improvement. This shift in mindset fosters resilience in the face of obstacles and encourages seeing failures as stepping stones toward something better.

Soft skills emerge as the unsung heroes of self-development – encompassing emotional intelligence, communication, adaptability, and leadership. These intangible assets set you apart, transforming you into not just a skilled professional but also an adaptable contributor capable of thriving in diverse environments. The investment in soft skills enhances your relationships, fosters effective collaboration, and positions you as someone who can excel in any setting.

Striking a balance between your personal and professional life becomes an integral part of this investment. It involves recognizing the importance of your mental and physical well-being. Regular self-assessment, mindfulness practices, and setting boundaries to prevent burnout are all facets of cultivating a healthy work-life balance. After all, what good is success without overall well-being?

In today's digital age, a wealth of online resources and platforms awaits exploration. Investing in digital literacy and leveraging online courses, webinars, and virtual communities expands your horizons. The democratization of information through digital channels means you can access knowledge and skills at your own pace, fostering a culture of lifelong learning.

The return on this investment extends beyond career advancement. It enriches your personal relationships, nurtures your creativity, and contributes to a sense of purpose and fulfillment. The self-awareness gained through continuous learning becomes a guiding force, aligning your personal values with your professional goals and creating a narrative that guides your decisions and actions.

Continuing with the exploration of personal strengths for strategic advantage is like navigating a dynamic dance, building upon the foundation of self-development and continuous learning. It is an ongoing process, not a one-time achievement – a melody of adaptability, collaboration, communication, and execution, with personal strengths serving as the instruments in this symphony.

Adaptability assumes the role of the main character in this narrative. It's not just about possessing a strength; it's about understanding how flexible it can be across different situations. For instance, if you excel at problem-solving, strategically applying this strength to decision-making, innovation, or scenarios requiring creative solutions demonstrates the breadth of its flexibility.

Collaboration emerges as a co-star. While your personal strengths are impressive, combining them with the strengths of others propels them to new heights. It's not a solo performance; it's about creating a collective advantage that surpasses what any individual could achieve alone. It's the magic that happens when diverse strengths come together. Effective communication rightfully takes center stage. Despite incredible strengths, if you can't express how they align with broader goals, their impact diminishes. Crafting a story that resonates – not just showcasing your strengths but strategically explaining why they matter – highlights the significance of communication. It serves as the bridge connecting your strengths with the bigger picture.

Adaptability, the main character, continues to shine. In a world that's always changing, the ability to pivot strategically is crucial. Your adaptability isn't a static trait; it's a dynamic force. Staying aware of trends, proactively seeking growth, and anticipating challenges represent strategic leverage of your adaptability.

Now, execution steps into the spotlight. All the strategy in the world doesn't mean much without effective implementation. Envisioning a brilliant strategy based on your strengths is one thing; execution is about turning that plan into tangible results. It's not just about imagining the path; it's about walking it with precision and impact.

Continuous refinement operates behind the scenes, making the entire performance seamless. It's a commitment to constant self-assessment, learning, and improvement. Embracing a growth mindset is not just a buzzword; it's a practical approach to evolving your strengths in response to new circumstances and opportunities.

So, this journey of strategic advantage is akin to being the conductor in an orchestra. Each personal strength is an instrument, and your role is to orchestrate the harmonious blend with the collective capabilities of those around you. It's not just about your solo; it's about creating a symphony where every note contributes to the richness of the collective melody.

Chapter 3

Navigating Wealth Creation

In the realm of wealth creation, individuals often embark on two primary routes: one as an intrapreneur and the other as an entrepreneur. Despite their distinct natures, these paths intertwine through threads of innovation, resilience, and the pursuit of opportunities.

An intrapreneur functions within the confines of an established organization, serving as a catalyst for change and innovation from within. Imagine an individual with an entrepreneurial mindset, operating within the secure framework of a pre-existing company. Intrapreneurs propel internal transformations, identifying growth opportunities, and introducing novel ideas to maintain the organization's competitiveness.

An intrapreneur's path revolves around recognizing avenues for innovation and enhancing efficiency within the current corporate framework. It requires a discerning vision for potential disruptions, a willingness to question established norms, and the skill to mobilize internal resources for transforming ideas into tangible outcomes. In essence, intrapreneurs transplant the entrepreneurial mindset into the organized setting of an established entity.

Now, shifting our focus to entrepreneurs – the designers of their fates in the business realm. Entrepreneurs dive into uncharted territories by founding and guiding their enterprises. They operate independently, making pivotal decisions, devising business models, and navigating the intricacies of business management. Essentially, entrepreneurs are risk-takers, embracing uncertainty to manifest their vision.

The entrepreneurial path is characterized by the liberty to innovate without the limitations of pre-existing corporate frameworks. Entrepreneurs undertake the responsibility of constructing something from scratch, starting from conceptualizing a business idea to obtaining funding and surmounting market challenges. It's a journey that requires strategic thinking, adept risk management, and a profound comprehension of market dynamics.

While operating in distinct contexts, intrapreneurs and entrepreneurs both build upon a shared foundation grounded in entrepreneurial principles: innovation, resilience, and the pursuit of opportunities. Intrapreneurs infuse innovation into established organizations, ensuring agility and competitiveness. Entrepreneurs, conversely, introduce creative solutions to meet market demands and propel economic advancement. It's crucial to recognize that the routes of intrapreneurship and entrepreneurship can intersect. Individuals may transition between both paths in their careers. An entrepreneur could assume an intrapreneurial position within a larger corporation, infusing their innovative mindset into an established environment. Conversely, an intrapreneur might choose to venture into entrepreneurship, aiming to transform their creative ideas into independent ventures.

When considering the trajectories of an intrapreneur and an entrepreneur, the key factor is aligning your journey with personal goals and values. Each path presents unique opportunities and challenges, and the decision ultimately hinges on what aligns with your aspirations and principles. Those leaning towards intrapreneurship typically opt for stability within the structure of a well-established organization. Intrapreneurs derive satisfaction from fostering innovation internally, utilizing the resources and support system of a company. This decision suits individuals who excel in collaborative settings, prioritize the security of an established entity, and perceive opportunities for personal growth within the confines of established corporate structures.

Conversely, the entrepreneurial journey appeals to those desiring autonomy, creative liberty, and a direct link between effort and results. Entrepreneurs are motivated by the desire to construct something distinctive, shape their own trajectory, and witness their vision come to life. This path is fitting for individuals who embrace the excitement of risk, appreciate handling various responsibilities, and are driven by the prospect of establishing a legacy through their independent venture. Yet, the decision isn't a straightforward one. It's a fluid choice shaped by personal circumstances, changing objectives, and the dynamic business environment. Some may discover satisfaction in moving between intrapreneurship and entrepreneurship during various phases of their careers, reaping the advantages of both realms.

Selecting a path in line with your goals and values requires self-reflection. What are your enduring aspirations? How comfortable are you with risk? Do you flourish in a structured setting, or do you yearn for the freedom to carve your own path? It's about comprehending your strengths, preferences, and identifying what provides you with a sense of purpose and fulfillment. Intrapreneurs derive fulfillment from aiding the expansion of a well-established organization, utilizing their skills to introduce positive change and innovation. The impact is significant but within the framework of a larger entity. In contrast, entrepreneurs revel in the challenge of constructing something anew, relishing the independence to chart their own path while also shouldering the responsibility for the success of their venture. The attractiveness of these journeys lies in their adaptability. Your goals and values may change, and so can your chosen path. It's not a universal decision; rather, it's a dynamic journey that adjusts to your personal and professional growth. A successful career doesn't always adhere to a linear path – it's about maneuvering through opportunities and challenges in a manner that aligns with your evolving goals and values.

In the end, whether you opt for intrapreneurship, entrepreneurship, or a combination at different career junctures, authenticity is paramount. It involves following a path that aligns with your values, enables you to achieve your goals, and imparts a sense of purpose to your professional journey. In the fabric of your career, the strands of intrapreneurship and entrepreneurship can intertwine to craft a distinctive and fulfilling narrative.

Chapter 4

The Profound Impact of Addressing Challenges

Embracing challenges is akin to unlocking a gateway to growth and self-discovery. Instead of perceiving challenges as obstacles, it involves seeing them as opportunities – a mindset that profoundly influences personal and professional advancement. When challenges present themselves, there exists a rich potential for learning, resilience, and innovation. It's not merely about surmounting obstacles; it's about recognizing that each challenge offers a chance to acquire new skills, broaden your perspective, and delve deep to uncover knowledge that might otherwise remain undiscovered.

This shift in mindset is grounded in the belief that adversity imparts valuable lessons. Confronted with difficulties, you're compelled to discover creative solutions, test your boundaries, and cultivate resilience that fortifies your character. It's a journey where each challenge transforms into a stepping stone, and you emerge with a wealth of wisdom that can only be gained through experience.

However, it goes beyond that – challenges act as catalysts for innovation. When faced with adversity, creativity tends to thrive. You're compelled to think unconventionally, explore uncharted territories, and devise solutions that have the potential to revolutionize the landscape. Challenges, viewed in this context, serve as the origin of groundbreaking ideas.

This journey isn't about evading discomfort; it's about embracing it. It involves recognizing that growth often occurs beyond the comfort zone. By confronting challenges directly, you cultivate a resilience that enables you to navigate uncertainties with grace and adaptability – qualities that become your secret weapon in both personal and professional spheres.

Furthermore, challenges serve as a mirror, encouraging self-reflection. They compel you to evaluate your strengths, confront your weaknesses, and pinpoint areas for enhancement. This introspection becomes a catalyst for ongoing self-improvement, nurturing a mindset of continuous learning. Each challenge transforms into an opportunity for personal and professional growth.

In the professional sphere, individuals who embrace challenges distinguish themselves as leaders. They become the go-to problem-solvers, adept at navigating complexities with a strategic mindset. Employers value professionals who not only address challenges but also view them as opportunities to enhance their skills and contribute to the overall success of the team or organization.

Embracing challenges fundamentally signifies a dedication to a growth mindset – acknowledging that obstacles are not roadblocks but rather the building blocks for success.

Sure, let's discuss cultivating problem-solving skills – it's akin to refining a superpower that not only aids in overcoming challenges but also establishes you as the person others turn to for solutions.

First and foremost, it begins with mindset. Instead of perceiving problems as insurmountable obstacles, view them as puzzles awaiting resolution. Foster a curiosity that motivates you to delve in, comprehend the intricacies, and explore every facet of the challenge.

Breaking problems into smaller components is crucial. It's akin to disassembling a complex issue into manageable segments. This approach provides a clear understanding of the situation, allowing you to address each part strategically.

Moreover, creativity serves as the secret ingredient. Problem-solving isn't a one-size-fits-all endeavor. You need to be receptive to thinking unconventionally, exploring alternative solutions, and acknowledging that there are multiple approaches to resolving a problem. Foster an environment that encourages diverse ideas – that's where innovation thrives.

Maintaining a methodical approach is crucial. Employing a structured method, whether it involves problem identification, information gathering, brainstorming solutions, or evaluating outcomes, ensures you stay organized. It's akin to having a roadmap for navigating through the intricacies of challenges.

Additionally, collaboration plays a vital role. Joining forces with others, exchanging ideas, and pooling intellectual resources often results in more robust solutions. It's not merely about gathering input; it's about actively listening, valuing diverse perspectives, and fostering an environment where everyone feels at ease sharing their thoughts. Adaptability is also a significant factor in achieving success. Remaining receptive to modifying your approach in response to feedback or new information is crucial. You're not inflexible; instead, you're adaptable, prepared to pivot and refine your strategies as the situation develops.

Constant learning is the driving force behind adept problem-solving. Each problem presents a new opportunity for exploration, and there's always more to discover. Whether it involves gaining fresh knowledge, extracting insights from previous experiences, or seeking guidance from mentors, the process of problem-solving is an ongoing pursuit of personal development.

In professional settings, possessing robust problem-solving skills elevates you to an invaluable position. You're not just identifying issues; you're an active member of the solution team. This skill stands out in leadership, project management, and any collaborative environment.

Cultivating problem-solving skills is akin to integrating resilience, innovation, and adaptability into the tapestry of your journey. It involves turning challenges into opportunities, addressing problems with curiosity and creativity, and actively playing a role in crafting solutions that influence your personal and professional achievements. It becomes your superhero cape in the grand adventure of growth.

Chapter 5

Cracking the Code for Sound Decision-Making

Alright, let's explore decision-making – a routine process we face daily, whether deciding what to have for breakfast or making crucial business choices. However, maneuvering through this terrain is no simple task. That's where a systematic approach becomes crucial – it's akin to having a reliable guide that assists you in navigating the complexities of decision-making with purpose and clarity.

To start, it's essential to have absolute clarity about the decision at hand. While it may seem fundamental, articulating the problem or goal establishes the foundation for all subsequent steps. It's akin to activating the GPS – you must know your destination before plotting the route.

Once you've clarified the decision, it's time to collect information. Information serves as your companion in decision-making. You take on the role of a detective, gathering data, conducting research, and seeking insights that illuminate the situation. In a world saturated with information, employing a systematic approach to sift through the noise ensures you're dealing with meaningful data.

Next, let's engage in brainstorming. A systematic approach prompts you to thoroughly explore your options. It's not about settling for the initial solution that comes to mind; rather, it involves contemplating various possibilities. This step infuses a creative element into the process, welcoming unconventional solutions.

Now that options are on the table, it's time for evaluation. This includes assessing each option against specific criteria, whether it's feasibility, cost, impact, or any other factors crucial in your context. Picture it as assigning scores to each option to determine the most favorable one. This introduces objectivity, aiding you in seeing beyond personal biases.

Remember the risk check. A systematic decision-making process includes foreseeing potential challenges. It involves questioning, "What could go wrong?" and preparing for it. This risk assessment ensures you're not taken by surprise and enables you to devise strategies to mitigate potential challenges.

Now, it's decision time. This is where you synthesize everything – the research, the brainstorming, the evaluation. It's the moment of choice, where you select the option that best aligns with your criteria and minimizes risks. It's the climax of the decision-making narrative.

However, there's more to it. Implementation follows. Making a decision is one aspect; translating it into action is another. A systematic approach involves planning how you'll execute your decision. It's about transforming your choice into an actionable plan, assigning responsibilities, and ensuring everyone is aware of the next steps.

The post-implementation evaluation serves as the epilogue. It's the phase where you reflect on your actions, compare them to your expectations, and identify any lessons to be learned. This feedback loop is vital for refining your approach in future decisions. It's the chapter of continuous improvement.

Let's delve into achieving the right equilibrium between intuition and data-driven approaches in decision-making. It's akin to having both a seasoned guide and a cutting-edge map – blending the wisdom of your instincts with the concrete insights offered by data. Striking this balance ensures decisions are not only well-informed but also carry the nuanced understanding that human intuition provides.

Intuition, often known as a "gut feeling," is that internal sense refined through experience, observations, and an innate grasp of situations. It's that subtle voice that imparts insights when confronted with uncertainty. While data-driven strategies rely on hard facts, figures, and statistical analysis, intuition introduces a qualitative dimension to decision-making.

The systematic method we explored earlier promotes collecting pertinent data, conducting extensive research, and impartially assessing options. However, this is where intuition comes into play – it contributes an additional layer of insight that may not be immediately evident in the numbers. It's the unspoken wisdom derived from years of navigating similar situations or comprehending nuances that might not be fully captured by data alone.

Achieving a balance between intuition and data-driven strategies requires recognizing the strengths and limitations of each. Data establishes a solid foundation, providing a clear view of trends, patterns, and probabilities. It is reliable and objective. In contrast, intuition introduces a subjective and experiential aspect. It involves tapping into your accumulated knowledge, identifying patterns that might elude the data, and making decisions based on a deeper understanding of the context.

In certain scenarios, the data might be unequivocal, firmly indicating a specific option.

However, there are instances where the data is unclear or lacking. This is where intuition becomes a valuable companion. It enables you to fill in the gaps, interpret the data in a broader context, and make decisions that encompass human elements like emotions, relationships, and cultural nuances.

Additionally, intuition can serve as an early warning system. It has the ability to sense when something doesn't quite align, even if the data appears favorable. It's that tingling feeling that encourages you to delve deeper, ask more questions, and ensure you're not overlooking critical aspects.

Think of it as a dance – data takes the lead with its structured steps, providing a solid framework for decision-making. Intuition follows, adding fluidity and adaptability to the routine. The key is to let them complement each other, not compete. When intuition and data work in harmony, decisions become well-rounded, considering both the empirical and nuanced aspects of a situation.

In an ever-evolving world, mastering the skill of balancing intuition and data-driven strategies is invaluable. It enables individuals and organizations to make decisions grounded in evidence yet flexible enough to adapt to unforeseen circumstances. It's about harnessing the power of both analytical and intuitive approaches to navigate the intricacies of decision-making with finesse.

Whether you're making choices about a marketing strategy, selecting a new team member, or guiding a project's direction, the collaboration between intuition and data-driven strategies guarantees that decisions are not only well-founded in theory but also resonate with the human touch that characterizes real-world situations. It's the fusion of the art and science of decision-making, working together to guarantee a balanced and comprehensive approach that can withstand the challenges of a dynamic and ever-evolving landscape.

Blueprint for Business success

Chapter 6

Crafting Your Collaborative Crew

Picture setting out on a voyage not as a lone navigator but amidst a vibrant team of individuals, each contributing distinct skills, experiences, and perspectives. This cooperative ethos lies at the core of triumph, be it in a workplace project, a community endeavor, or a personal undertaking. Let's explore why collaboration and team building transcend mere workplace terminology to become essential components that enhance our shared capabilities. Collaboration resembles conducting a symphony with a variety of talents. It recognizes that each individual contributes a unique note to the composition. When these notes blend in harmony, the outcome is a melody that surpasses the richness, nuance, and captivation of any solo performance. Diversity here is not merely about fulfilling checkboxes; it's about accessing a collective intelligence that propels us beyond individual achievements.

Envision a team engaging in brainstorming to solve a intricate problem. It's akin to a puzzle where each team member possesses a crucial piece. Through collaboration, these pieces effortlessly interlock, revealing a complete picture that goes beyond the constraints of individual viewpoints. This is the magical synergy that emerges when diverse strengths converge, propelling the team toward inventive solutions.

Collaboration serves as the catalyst for innovation. It involves the convergence of ideas, the clash of perspectives, and a readiness to challenge established norms. When people from diverse backgrounds collaborate, they introduce a spectrum of creativity. This diversity acts as a driving force for breakthroughs, pushing the limits of what can be achieved and propelling progress forward.

Now, let's delve into team building – the skill of molding a collection of individuals into a unified entity. It goes beyond mere physical presence in a room; it involves establishing an environment where trust, respect, and effective communication thrive. A proficiently built team isn't merely an assemblage; it forms a cohesive unit where each member comprehends their role, appreciates contributions, and is dedicated to shared objectives.

In the business domain, proficient team building forms the foundation of efficiency. Trust and backing among team members streamline collaboration, fostering a shared vision, clear communication, and a collective commitment to success. This unity diminishes friction, streamlines decision-making, and hastens the accomplishment of goals.

Outside the workplace, collaboration and team building are crucial in community initiatives and personal pursuits. Whether orchestrating a local event, initiating a creative project, or participating in charitable activities, the underlying principles remain consistent. Collaboration cultivates a community sense and shared responsibility, magnifying the influence of collective endeavors.

In today's interconnected global landscape, where challenges necessitate diverse expertise, collaboration and team building are not merely optional – they are imperative. The complexity of contemporary issues often exceeds the scope of individual solutions. It's the merging of minds, skills, and experiences through collaboration that establishes a robust foundation for addressing these challenges.

Creating and guiding an exceptional team is akin to conducting a symphony. It demands finesse, a profound understanding of each instrument's distinctive sound, and the ability to unite them in harmony. In the realm of collaboration and team building, effective leadership serves as the guiding force. Let's explore strategies that not only aid in assembling exceptional teams but also steer them towards greatness.

Firstly, envision your team as a varied playlist. Instead of identical notes, strive for a mix that complements one another. Diversity goes beyond being a trendy term; it's the catalyst igniting innovation, enabling your team to approach challenges from diverse angles.

Open communication functions as the recurring melody throughout this composition. Establishing an environment where everyone feels at ease sharing ideas and feedback is crucial. When your team comprehends the overarching vision and the relevance of their contributions, it fosters a sense of belonging and commitment.

Clear goals serve as the musical sheet for your team's performance. They must know their direction and expectations. Goals should be both challenging and attainable, guiding the team like North Stars to keep them on course and motivated.

Leadership isn't about being a maestro; it's about enabling. Provide your team with necessary resources, support their decisions, and empower them to take the lead. Autonomy not only uplifts morale but taps into the intrinsic motivation that drives high performance.

Foster a culture of collaboration and respect. In an atmosphere where team members trust each other, freely exchange ideas, and genuinely value contributions, magic happens. This collaborative culture becomes the breeding ground for creativity and positivity.

Don't overlook applauding the solos. Acknowledge and celebrate individual and team achievements, whether through formal recognition programs or a simple shout-out. Recognizing success reinforces camaraderie and a sense of accomplishment.

Investing in professional development is akin to tuning your instruments. Keep your team sharp and updated through training and learning opportunities, ensuring adaptability, dynamism, and staying at the forefront of their field. Conflict resolution is an integral part of the score. Address conflicts openly and constructively; turning conflicts into opportunities for growth is a hallmark of effective leadership. It's about maintaining the rhythm even when things deviate a bit.

Lastly, lead by example. Showcase the values, work ethic, and dedication you expect from your team. When your team witnesses you embodying the principles of collaboration and commitment, it sets a standard motivating them to strive for excellence.

In the realm of fostering high-performance teams, trust emerges as the vital component that binds everything together. Within the team, the focus lies in cultivating an environment where everyone experiences acknowledgment and value. Open and transparent communication takes center stage, ensuring that everyone stays informed, shares updates, and openly discusses challenges.

Reliability serves as the adhesive that unites the team. Each member consistently fulfilling promises builds a foundation of confidence and trust. Additionally, empathy plays a crucial role – understanding each other's needs fosters a supportive atmosphere conducive to the thriving of trust. Recognition becomes a catalyst; celebrating individual and team achievements acts as fuel for trust, sustaining positive vibes.

When it comes to stakeholders, the emphasis shifts towards extending trust and credibility. Transparency becomes paramount – openly communicating the current status, potential risks, and any alterations in plans. Timely responses convey to stakeholders their significance, while aligning goals establishes a sense of partnership.

Proactively addressing challenges demonstrates the team's dedication to finding solutions. Building trust is akin to nurturing a relationship – it demands continuous effort, authentic communication, and a touch of celebration. It serves as the foundational element propelling collaborations to flourish, transforming a mere group of individuals into a cohesive, high-performing team. Whether within the team or with stakeholders, the reminder persists that trust is the magical ingredient making everything function seamlessly.

In the domain of high-performing teams, trust and reliability intricately weave the threads of connections, elevating collaboration beyond a functional aspect to an art form. Envision a team where each member not only contributes their skills but shares a collective belief in each other's reliability. It surpasses meeting deadlines;

it's about the assurance that when faced with challenges, teammates are steadfast in their support. This sense of trust metamorphoses a group into a close-knit unit, where decision-making flows effortlessly, and creativity knows no bounds.

Reliable relationships within the team transcend mere coexistence – they represent a symphony of skills in harmony, a convergence of ideas in dance, and a chorus of voices celebrating both triumphs and challenges. It becomes the intangible force driving the team forward, transforming them not merely into a collection of individuals but into a collective force greater than the sum of its parts.

As the team extends its collaborative spirit to stakeholders, a magical transformation unfolds. Stakeholders cease being external entities; they become integral partners in a shared journey.

Transparency and openness become brushstrokes illustrating a vivid picture of progress, challenges, and solutions. Timely and consistent updates compose the rhythm of a reliable relationship with stakeholders, creating a melody resonating with understanding and shared objectives.

Harmonizing business objectives with stakeholder expectations resembles discovering the ideal chord – a resonance that signifies collective triumph. Stakeholders place trust not solely in deliverables but in the entire journey, confident that your team is finely tuned to their needs and aspirations. This partnership is rooted in mutual respect, understanding, and a commitment to navigating the ever-evolving business landscape together. Robust relationships, whether within the team or with stakeholders, transcend merely expediting business success; they redefine it. These connections inject resilience into the team's DNA, enabling it not only to navigate challenges but to embrace them as avenues for growth. Amidst the dynamic business dance, where uncertainty prevails, these relationships emerge as the anchor, the compass, and the driving force propelling businesses towards sustained success. They epitomize the human touch in the corporate realm, where connections transcend transactions and represent a shared journey characterized by trust, understanding, and the assurance of mutual success.

Blueprint for Business success

Chapter 7

Rapid Expansion Strategies

Envision expanding your business is akin to conducting a symphony, where every element plays a role in the cohesive expansion of your enterprise. It starts with a meticulously planned strategy, akin to a guiding melody that unites everyone within the organization toward common objectives. Picture it as arranging the stage for a performance where each action is purposeful and adds to the overarching composition.

Effectiveness transforms into your rhythmic foundation – optimizing internal procedures, automating when feasible, establishing a seamless and effective workflow. It's akin to discovering the ideal tempo that propels the entire team ahead, guaranteeing synchronization. Technology serves as your behind-the-scenes team, diligently aiding the primary performance. Committing to a scalable technological infrastructure is comparable to having state-of-the-art sound equipment – it effortlessly adjusts to the rising demands of an expanding audience.

Broadening your impact resembles bringing your music to novel venues. This entails delving into diverse markets, comprehending varied audiences, and customizing your offerings to strike a chord with them. It involves connecting with new listeners who resonate with your distinctive melody. Strategic collaborations are akin to joining forces with other musicians. Each contributes their own expertise, fashioning a more intricate and enriched composition. It's a collaborative energy that broadens your influence by accessing established networks and audiences. Digital marketing serves as your spotlight, casting light on your presence on the expansive stage of the internet. Through social media, compelling content, and strategic SEO, you become the main attraction, attracting a wider audience eager to witness your performance.

Client relationships embody your devoted enthusiasts, cheering you on through every composition. While gaining new admirers is essential, retaining those who have been with you from the start is equally paramount. Satisfied enthusiasts evolve into your brand advocates, spreading the word and guaranteeing your return for an encore.

Investing in your team's skills and development is comparable to refining instruments before a significant performance. Continuous learning ensures their ability to navigate the intricacies of an expanding presentation, adapting to the evolving tempo and rhythm. Data analytics functions as your conductor's baton, directing your decisions with precision. It involves gauging the audience, understanding their preferences, and making real-time adjustments to maintain a flawless and resonant performance. Crafting a robust financial plan resembles budgeting for a tour – guaranteeing ample resources to elevate your performance. Close monitoring of financial metrics enables adjustments, ensuring a seamless continuation of the show.

For those seeking to expand their act to new cities, franchising or licensing mirrors sharing your sheet music with other artists. It's a means to replicate your success in fresh locations, broadening your fanbase and introducing your unique sound to diverse audiences.

Navigating the business growth landscape is akin to orchestrating a vibrant symphony, each phase bringing unique challenges and opportunities – a dynamic composition requiring meticulous preparation and attentiveness to the evolving melody. As the music of growth unfolds, anticipating challenges is crucial, akin to fine-tuning harmonies in a complex piece. Operational strain may emerge, introducing a discordant note within the organization. The objective is to refine operational strategies, ensuring the tempo of growth doesn't disrupt harmony. Scaling costs present another facet, necessitating a well-calibrated financial strategy to synchronize with the expanding demands of the business score. Talent acquisition assumes a solo role, a delicate performance to find the right notes for the growing ensemble. It involves anticipating the needs of the expanding team, fostering a melody of collaboration, and ensuring each team member contributes harmoniously. Persistent competition serves as a counterpoint, urging businesses to navigate the competitive landscape with vigilance, market analysis, and innovative variations to maintain a distinctive tune. Yet, within challenges lies a symphony of opportunities. Expanding into new markets becomes a movement of exploration, introducing fresh motifs into the composition. It's about playing with different notes, conducting thorough market research, and harmonizing offerings with the unique needs of diverse customer segments. Innovation and diversification become a lively interlude, an opportunity to introduce new rhythms into the symphony. It's about embracing creativity, exploring novel melodies, and creating variations that resonate with the evolving audience. Strategic partnerships take center stage, acting as a powerful chorus that enhances the overall composition. It involves collaborating with other businesses, harmonizing strengths, and expanding the ensemble to reach new heights. Building a resilient foundation transforms into a steady rhythm, a reliable beat that ensures the symphony endures challenges and seizes opportunities. Scalable systems are the supporting harmonies, adapting seamlessly to the changing tempo of growth. Leadership development becomes a solo performance, nurturing the conductors and musicians guiding the ensemble through the complexities of expansion. Agile decision-making becomes a dynamic tempo, allowing the symphony to respond swiftly to changes in the business landscape. Risk management serves as a protective harmony, identifying and mitigating potential disruptions to keep the symphony playing smoothly.

In the narrative of organizational growth, cultivating a values-driven culture is akin to composing a song that reverberates throughout every facet of the company. It goes beyond mere regulations on paper; it's about imbuing the organization with a soul, a set of principles that animate every action and decision. Picture it as crafting a distinctive melody where each note symbolizes a core value, establishing the rhythm for the entire composition. These values aren't just words; they are the essence that defines our identity. Conveying these values is like a conductor guiding an orchestra, ensuring every member plays in harmony with the established principles.

Leadership takes center stage as the primary conductor, embodying the values and setting the tone for everyone else. It transcends merely articulating principles, as it involves living them, inspiring others to follow the melody of shared values. Leadership becomes the propelling force that advances our collective endeavors.

In this symphony of values, employee engagement emerges as the vibrant melody, where individuals discover purpose aligning their personal values with those of the organization. It revolves around fostering an environment where everyone feels a sense of belonging, recognizing how their unique contributions fit into the broader picture. Decision-making transforms into a collaborative composition, guided by the values forming the foundation of our culture. It entails contemplating the impact on all involved, making choices resonant with our principles, and ensuring each decision contributes to the overall harmony.

Adaptation becomes a dynamic element of the melody, acknowledging that our values may require adjustment as the business landscape evolves. It's about staying attuned to the world around us, embracing fresh perspectives, and fine-tuning our cultural melody to remain in harmony with the changing times. Recognition and appreciation constitute the emotional crescendos, celebrating individuals and teams embodying our values. It's about reinforcing the positive notes, fostering a culture where living by the values is not just anticipated but acknowledged and celebrated.

Chapter 8

Crafting Systems for Effective Business Tracking

Establishing efficient systems to monitor business performance is akin to forging a reliable compass for navigating the journey of success. It involves creating a tool that not only scrutinizes your operations closely but also furnishes valuable insights to help you traverse the ever-shifting landscape. Envision it as assembling a finely tuned instrument that seamlessly syncs with the heartbeat of your business. The initial step is identifying key performance indicators (KPIs) – these are akin to the musical notes on your sheet, representing the metrics that genuinely matter for your business. Selecting the right technology resembles a solo performance. It's the technology that transforms raw data into actionable insights – whether it's advanced analytics tools, user-friendly data visualization platforms, or integrated software solutions.

Collecting data serves as the consistent rhythm that guarantees your tracking systems capture the intricacies of your business operations. It involves establishing processes that seamlessly gather, organize, and store pertinent data, creating a continuous beat for informed decision-making.

Collaboration between departments forms the harmonious ensemble, interconnecting various facets of your business into a unified performance. Dismantling organizational silos constructs a symphony where each department contributes to the overall melody, providing a comprehensive perspective on your business's performance.

Consistent analysis is a continuous composition, deciphering the gathered data and converting it into practical insights. This process involves grasping the story within the numbers, recognizing trends, and making informed decisions to improve your business performance. Adaptability serves as the improvisational element, acknowledging the dynamic nature of the business landscape. Your monitoring systems should possess flexibility, adapting to changes and evolving with the market's shifting rhythms. Conveying insights acts as the resonant chord, guaranteeing that valuable information reaches the intended audience. This involves translating intricate data into understandable narratives, empowering key stakeholders to make well-informed decisions. Through effective communication, your monitoring systems shift from being mere instruments to becoming impactful storytellers.

Constructing efficient systems to monitor business performance transcends mere technicality; it involves an artistic orchestration that seamlessly integrates technology, data, and strategy into a harmonious composition. When executed with care, these systems not only oversee performance but also actively contribute to the symphony of success, steering your business towards its crescendo.

Leveraging data for informed decision-making is akin to possessing a reliable guidebook that assists in navigating the complexities of business choices. It goes beyond the accumulation of data; instead, it involves revealing valuable insights that serve as a compass, guiding you toward the most strategic paths.

Imagine peeling away the layers of a captivating story. The initial phase involves gathering a diverse array of pertinent data points – the raw material that shapes the narrative of your decision-making journey. It's akin to collecting clues to grasp the complete picture of what's transpiring. Analyzing the data is comparable to being a detective, diligently seeking patterns and connections that may not be immediately evident. The goal is to transform raw data into practical insights that facilitate an understanding of nuances, identification of trends, and anticipation of potential challenges. This analytical phase serves as the linchpin for unlocking the true value embedded in your data. The subsequent phase involves interpreting the findings, transitioning into the storytelling phase. Once the data undergoes analysis, the focus shifts to crafting a narrative that makes sense. What revelations does the data unveil about your business story? How do the insights align with your objectives? It's about translating the intricacies of data into a lucid and compelling tale that guides decision-makers. In this narrative, decision-makers assume leading roles. Armed with insights from the data, they step into the spotlight to make informed decisions. This entails comprehending the implications of the data, contemplating various scenarios, and selecting a course of action that closely aligns with the strategic direction of the business. The execution of decisions becomes the unfolding drama, where choices informed by data insights transform into real-world strategies. It involves implementing the selected plans, monitoring their impact, and making adjustments as necessary. The implementation phase completes the narrative loop, providing feedback that contributes to the ongoing story of your business.

Embracing continuous learning and improvement serves as the subsequent chapters, acknowledging the perpetual evolution of the business story. It involves collecting feedback from decision outcomes, refining strategies based on real-world results, and ensuring that the subsequent chapters of your business narrative are even more compelling.

Chapter 9

A Strategic Leader Stays Wary at All Times

Maintaining a watchful eye in the dynamic business landscape is akin to cultivating a garden undergoing continuous changes. It involves adopting a strategic mindset that recognizes the importance of staying alert and adaptable amid the evolving challenges and opportunities. Imagine it as tending to a garden where conditions are constantly shifting. The initial step is to regularly scan the horizon, observing market trends, competitor actions, and emerging technologies. This vigilance is comparable to understanding external factors that can influence your business ecosystem, akin to caring for the soil to ensure its well-being.

Foreseeing potential disruptions is similar to pruning the branches in gardening. This entails identifying weak points, assessing vulnerabilities, and proactively addressing areas susceptible to challenges. This proactive approach allows for strategic preparation, ensuring your business remains resilient in the face of unforeseen circumstances. Regular risk assessments function as the meticulous cultivation of a thriving landscape, involving the evaluation of potential threats and opportunities. Understanding their impact and making informed decisions enable navigation through the dynamic terrain, ensuring your business stays agile and responsive to the changing environment. Adapting to market shifts mirrors adjusting gardening techniques based on seasonal changes, involving fine-tuning strategies, revisiting business plans, and pivoting when necessary. This adaptability ensures that your business not only survives but thrives amidst market fluctuations.

Sustaining open channels of communication is akin to consistent watering that fosters growth. This entails staying connected with stakeholders, customers, and employees, actively listening to their feedback, and comprehending the pulse of the market. This continual dialogue ensures that your business stays in tune with the needs and expectations of its ecosystem.

Pouring resources into technology and innovation is like introducing robust, new plant varieties. It involves embracing tools and methodologies that boost efficiency, refine processes, and position your business at the forefront of industry trends. This investment serves as a catalyst for sustained growth in the ever-changing business environment. Vigilance in a dynamic business setting isn't about residing in constant fear; it's a strategic dedication to staying informed, agile, and prepared. It acknowledges that, similar to a garden, a business demands continual attention, adaptation, and a sharp awareness of its surroundings to thrive amid the shifting seasons of the marketplace.

Discussing the proactive navigation of changing landscapes involves staying ahead and anticipating shifts in the industry, akin to navigating uncharted waters. It's a journey that requires foresight, adaptability, and a profound understanding of the changing currents within your business domain.

Consider it as navigating a ship across unpredictable seas. To start, you must maintain a vigilant gaze on the horizon, monitoring market trends, technological advancements, and evolving customer preferences – akin to scanning the vast ocean for potential changes and challenges on the horizon. Networking and collaboration function like a reliable crew, working in unison to navigate unknown waters. Building partnerships, participating in industry discussions, and collaborating with others offer insights and early warnings about forthcoming shifts. This collaborative effort ensures you have a network of allies to navigate the complex currents of industry changes. Investing in research and development becomes an exploration of uncharted territories. This entails allocating resources to understand emerging technologies, market dynamics, and potential disruptors. This investment in exploration equips your business with the knowledge and tools

92

required to sail through the unknown and stay ahead of industry shifts. Customer feedback and market intelligence serve as the compass guiding your journey. Regularly collecting feedback, monitoring social trends, and analyzing market data are essential navigation tools. This feedback loop ensures your business stays attuned to the changing needs and expectations of your audience, allowing you to adjust your course accordingly. Remaining agile is akin to having a responsive sail that adjusts to changing winds. Establishing a flexible organizational structure, fostering a culture of innovation, and promoting adaptive leadership enable your business to swiftly respond to industry shifts. This agility ensures your ship can navigate through turbulent changes with ease.

Imagine scenario planning as the strategic roadmap guiding you through potential challenges. This process entails envisioning various future scenarios, evaluating their potential impact on your business, and formulating strategies to navigate each one. Embracing this forward-thinking approach equips your business with a comprehensive plan for different possibilities, enabling you to stay ahead and resilient in the face of uncertainty.

Continuous learning and skill development serve as the continual training of your crew. When you invest in the knowledge and capabilities of your team, you ensure that they are well-prepared to handle new challenges and adeptly navigate through industry changes. This dedication to ongoing learning positions your business as a skilled and proficient navigator in the ever-changing business landscape.

Blueprint for Business success

Chapter 10

Outsmarting Giants and Steering the Storyline

Competing with larger rivals is akin to venturing into unfamiliar territory. While it poses challenges, smaller businesses can not only compete but also flourish in the market with the right strategies. Here are some people-centric approaches to establish a strong presence against industry giants:

Specialize in What You Love: Rather than attempting to cater to everyone, concentrate on what you're passionate about and become a specialist in that particular niche. While larger competitors may adopt a broad approach, you

96

can excel by providing specialized solutions tailored to a specific audience.

Quick Moves, Smart Decisions: Picture yourself as an agile dancer on the market stage. Utilize your nimbleness to make decisions promptly. While larger players may face bureaucratic obstacles, your capacity to adapt swiftly can be a notable advantage.

Know Your Customers Like Friends: View your customers as friends, not mere transactions. Leverage your smaller size to foster personal connections. Harness this intimacy to gain a deeper understanding of their needs, providing a personalized experience that larger corporations might find challenging.

Unleash Your Creative Spirit: Consider your business as a canvas. Embrace creativity and innovation, utilizing your flexibility to experiment and introduce novel ideas that can distinguish you from others.

Build Allies in the Business Realm: Establish partnerships as if assembling a dream team. Engage in strategic collaborations to amplify your strengths. Through collective efforts, you gain access to resources that may extend beyond your individual capabilities.

Shine Online with Digital Magic: Envision your online presence as a dynamic mural. Utilize digital marketing to narrate your story. Employ social media, content creation, and strategic SEO approaches to compete effectively in the digital arena.

Give Customer Service a Hug: Approach customer service as if you're inviting guests into your home. Strive to exceed expectations in building loyalty. Your personalized approach has the potential to foster a connection that larger corporations may find challenging to establish.

Master the Art of Efficiency: Become a astute financial conductor. Maintain lean and efficient operations. Your skill in intelligently managing costs ensures competitiveness in the financial arena.

Cultivate a Workplace Symphony: Envision your workplace as a symphony of harmony. Cultivate a positive culture that draws in and retains top talent. A closely connected team can nurture innovation and enhance productivity.

Be a Lifelong Learner: See yourself as an eternal learner in the business realm. Maintain curiosity and stay well-informed. Adapting to market dynamics positions you ahead of the curve, showcasing that you're not merely enduring but flourishing.

Ultimately, success is not determined by size; it's about infusing your business with passion and dedication. Embrace your distinctive strengths, move to your unique beat, and compete against industry giants, scripting your triumph in the business arena.

Shaping and steering your business narrative is like assuming the role of the storyteller for your unique journey. It's more than just outlining your actions; it involves narrating the emotions, plot twists, and lessons learned. Here's a guide on how to artfully weave and navigate your business narrative.

Let's delve into the art of crafting and managing your business narrative. Imagine your business story as an engaging novel. Identify its essence – the inspiration behind the business, the obstacles overcome, and the unique elements that make your story unforgettable. Begin with the opening chapter, narrating the origin of your business. Share the passion and vision that ignited its creation, portraying it as a tale of determination with challenges and valuable lessons. Make sure your audience connects with the human side of your journey.

In your business narrative, your team and customers play crucial roles as characters. Emphasize their personalities, talents, and stories within your organization. Showcase how these individuals contribute to the overarching plot, forming meaningful relationships that propel the narrative forward.

In the storytelling of your business narrative, view challenges as plot twists that add depth and intrigue. Describe the navigation through tough times, detailing the decisions made and showcasing resilience. Integrate these challenges into the storyline, emphasizing growth and adaptability. Frame your successes as triumphant moments in the narrative. Share both significant and minor victories, celebrating milestones with your audience. By doing so, you make them feel like an integral part of the narrative, creating pivotal chapters that build excitement and engagement.

Picture consistency as the recurring theme woven into your narrative. Maintain uniform messaging, brand image, and values across all platforms, creating a coherent and memorable story that resonates with your audience.

Envision your business narrative as an ongoing conversation. Engage with your audience through social media, surveys, and feedback, actively listening to their responses and integrating their input into your story. This dialogue strengthens the connection between your brand and your audience.

Consider your business narrative as a dynamic storyline, allowing it to evolve and adapt with the changing business landscape. Embrace new chapters, innovations, and expansions, as a narrative that reflects growth and evolution captures the interest of your audience. Regard transparency as the cornerstone of your narrative. Be open about your business processes, challenges, and successes, as this transparency builds trust with your audience, making them feel like insiders in your story.

Envision your business's future as the epilogue of the narrative. Share your vision, goals, and aspirations, inviting your audience to be part of the next chapters in your story. This forward-looking perspective keeps your narrative alive and engaging.

Chapter 11

Strategic Maestros

Mastering sales, negotiation, and influence goes beyond mere transactions; it's a nuanced journey involving relationship-building, understanding human dynamics, and honing communication skills. In this exploration, we dissect each skill set, unveiling the strategies and nuances essential for proficiency.

Building Relationships, Not Just Transactions

Salesmanship transcends mere deal closure; it's a profound interaction where trust, understanding, and value intertwine. Successful sales professionals navigate this landscape by prioritizing relationship-building over transactional gains.

Understanding the Customer: Successful sales initiation begins with a thorough comprehension of the customer. This entails active listening, posing pertinent questions, and empathizing with their needs. The objective is to craft a personalized experience that aligns with the customer's distinct requirements.

Crafting Compelling Narratives: Each product or service possesses its narrative. Proficient sales professionals excel in constructing engaging stories that highlight the benefits and solutions provided. It involves creating a vivid picture that aligns with the customer's aspirations and challenges..

Embracing Consultative Selling: Traditional pushy sales tactics are a thing of the past. In the present, consultative selling takes the lead. This method entails adopting a consultant role rather than that of a salesperson, guiding customers through their decision-making process and providing customized solutions.

Navigating Objections with Finesse: Objections should be seen as opportunities, not obstacles. A proficient salesperson adeptly handles objections, using them as stepping stones toward achieving a successful sale.

Follow-up and Relationship Maintenance: Finalizing a deal marks the start of a new chapter. Accomplished sales professionals emphasize post-sale relationships, maintaining regular follow-ups, delivering ongoing value, and promptly addressing customer needs to foster long-term loyalty.

Finding Win-Win Solutions

Negotiation is a complex interplay of compromise, assertiveness, and creativity. It transcends mere haggling, aiming to discover solutions that satisfy both parties involved.

Preparation as the Foundation: Thorough preparation is crucial before entering a negotiation. This involves comprehending the other party's needs, articulating your objectives clearly, and foreseeing potential compromises, setting the stage for a successful negotiation.

Active Listening and Empathy: Listening isn't merely a passive aspect of negotiation; it serves as a strategic tool. Engaging in active listening and expressing empathy fosters a collaborative environment, with a fundamental emphasis on comprehending the other party's perspective to achieve a mutually beneficial agreement.

Effective Communication: Clear and articulate communication is crucial during negotiations. Expressing your needs, expectations, and concessions with clarity helps prevent misunderstandings and promotes transparency.

Building Rapport and Trust: Negotiation is a human endeavor, and establishing rapport and trust with the other party can profoundly impact the negotiation process. Trust creates an environment conducive to open communication and collaborative problem-solving.

Flexibility and Adaptability: A proficient negotiator demonstrates flexibility and adaptability. Recognizing that circumstances may evolve during negotiations, the ability to pivot while maintaining focus on the ultimate objective is a distinguishing feature of negotiation expertise.

Creative Problem-Solving: Negotiation frequently involves devising inventive solutions for intricate issues. Engaging in creative thinking, exploring alternatives, and suggesting innovative compromises all play a role in achieving successful negotiations.

The Art of Persuasion

Mastering the skill of persuasion involves comprehending psychological triggers, utilizing ethical persuasion techniques etc. Influence is the subtle force that shapes decisions without resorting to overt coercion.

Understanding Psychological Triggers: The art of influence frequently relies on understanding and leveraging psychological triggers, such as reciprocity, social proof, authority, consistency, liking, and scarcity. Ethically utilizing these triggers enhances one's persuasive abilities.

Establishing Credibility and Authority: The power of influence is heightened when combined with credibility and authority. Demonstrating expertise in the field, showcasing relevant experience, and offering valuable insights all contribute to an increased level of influence.

Ethical Persuasion Techniques: Authentic influence adheres to ethical standards. Persuasive techniques that honor the autonomy and well-being of others establish a reputation for trustworthiness. While manipulation may result in short-term gains, ethical persuasion ensures lasting influence.

Adaptability to Different Personality Types: Recognizing the diversity among people calls for varied influence strategies. Tailoring one's approach to different personality types showcases emotional intelligence and boosts the impact of influence.

Blending the intricate skills of sales, negotiation, and influence is the pivotal element for achieving strategic business success. These skills form a dynamic triad that collaborates harmoniously to propel your business forward amidst the continuously changing business landscape.

Mastering sales serves as the foundation for strategic success, nurturing a customer-centric approach that drives organic growth, extends into new markets, and adjusts to emerging industry trends. It's a dynamic perspective where the relationships formed during the sales process evolve into the cornerstone for repeat business and referrals.

Expertise in negotiation stands as the linchpin for collaborative success, reaching beyond deal closure to cultivate strategic partnerships, streamline the supply chain, and facilitate nimble problem-solving. Your adept negotiation skills position your business as a flexible problem solver, ensuring resilience in the face of challenges.

Mastery in influence molds business culture and influence, establishing thought leadership, constructing a brand with integrity, and nurturing employee engagement and innovation. It involves leaving a lasting impact on the industry, community, and perceptions associated with your brand. Your brand becomes synonymous with expertise, transparency, and ethical influence.

The strategic fusion of these skills generates a synergy that propels your business to unprecedented heights. It goes beyond mere transactions; it's about fostering sustainable growth, achieving collaborative success, and leaving a lasting imprint on the business landscape. Envision these skills not as standalone tools but as interconnected threads weaving a narrative of excellence, where mastering these skills serves as the compass directing your business toward strategic success.

Conclusion

As we conclude this shared journey, view your foray into strategic business not as a final endpoint but as an ongoing narrative—each segment filled with challenges to conquer, victories to applaud, and an unwavering pursuit of excellence. The skills we've delved into are more than just tools; they are your reliable companions guiding you through the ever-changing realm of strategic pursuits. Maintain the belief that your business is not a static entity but a living, evolving force capable of growth and adaptation. Embrace challenges as chances for innovation, setbacks as lessons, and consider the commitment to continual learning as the pulse of your success.

Picture your business not merely as a participant but as a trendsetter, a influential voice shaping the industry landscape. The strategic incorporation of these skills positions you not just as a participant but as a leader, shaping success in the ever-evolving business arena. As you conclude this chapter and turn towards the future, let the encouragement for ongoing growth resonate within you. The pages ahead are blank, ready for your distinct story of new ventures, partnerships, and transformative narratives. This isn't just the conclusion of a book; it's a roadmap for creating a legacy in the business world.

May your journey be characterized by sustained success, groundbreaking achievements, and a lasting impact on the industry. Keep pushing boundaries, honing your skills, and carving the path toward strategic excellence. Here's to your continual growth and success in the unfolding narrative of strategic business endeavors.

Leaving a Review

Dear Reader,

I hope this message finds you well. I want to express my sincere gratitude for choosing to explore the content of this book. The journey has been truly remarkable, and I genuinely hope the insights within the book have been beneficial to you.

As the author, your feedback is of great significance to me. It would be an honor if you could take a moment to share your thoughts and impressions by leaving a review at the place where you acquired the book.

Your review not only provides valuable insights for me but also serves as a guide for fellow readers, helping them determine if the book aligns with their needs and interests. Whether you opt for a brief commentary or a more detailed reflection, your honest feedback is highly appreciated.

Thank you once again for being a part of this literary journey. I look forward to hearing your thoughts and genuinely appreciate the time and consideration you invest in this.

Warm regards,

Lane J. Taylor